NATIVE AMERICAN NATIONS

THE OJIBWE

BY BETTY MARCKS

CONSULTANT: TIM TOPPER, CHEYENNE RIVER SIOUX

BLASTOFF! DISCOVERY

BELLWETHER MEDIA • MINNEAPOLIS, MN

Author's Statement of Positionality:
I am a white woman of European descent. As such, I can claim no direct lived experience of being a Native American. In writing this book, I have tried to be an ally by relying on sources by Native American writers and authors whenever possible and have worked to let their voices guide its content.

This edition first published in 2025 by Bellwether Media, Inc.

No part of this publication may be reproduced in whole or in part without written permission of the publisher. For information regarding permission, write to Bellwether Media, Inc.,
Attention: Permissions Department,
6012 Blue Circle Drive, Minnetonka, MN 55343.

Library of Congress Cataloging-in-Publication Data

Names: Marcks, Betty, author.
Title: The Ojibwe / by Betty Marcks.
Description: Minneapolis, MN : Bellwether Media, 2025. | Series: Blastoff! discovery: Native American nations | Includes bibliographical references and index.
  | Audience: Ages 7-13 | Audience: Grades 4-6 | Summary: "Engaging images accompany information about the Ojibwe people. The combination of high-interest subject matter and narrative text is intended for students in grades 3 through 8" – Provided by publisher.
Identifiers: LCCN 2024016015 (print) | LCCN 2024016016 (ebook) | ISBN 9798893040098 (library binding) | ISBN 9798893041514 (paperback) | ISBN 9781644879412 (ebook)
Subjects: LCSH: Ojibwa Indians–Juvenile literature.
Classification: LCC E99.C6 (print) | LCC E99.C6 (ebook) |
  DDC 977.004/97333–dc23/eng/20240513
LC record available at https://lccn.loc.gov/2024016015
LC ebook record available at https://lccn.loc.gov/2024016016

Text copyright © 2025 by Bellwether Media, Inc. BLASTOFF! DISCOVERY and associated logos are trademarks and/or registered trademarks of Bellwether Media, Inc. Bellwether Media is a division of Chrysalis Education Group.

Editor: Elizabeth Neuenfeldt   Series Designer: Andrea Schneider
Book Designer: Laura Sowers

Printed in the United States of America, North Mankato, MN.

TABLE OF CONTENTS

THE ORIGINAL PEOPLE	4
TRADITIONAL OJIBWE LIFE	6
EUROPEAN CONTACT	12
LIFE TODAY	16
CONTINUING TRADITIONS	20
FIGHT TODAY, BRIGHT TOMORROW	24
TIMELINE	28
GLOSSARY	30
TO LEARN MORE	31
INDEX	32

THE ORIGINAL PEOPLE

The Ojibwe are a Native American nation. In the Ojibwe language, people are called *Anishinaabe*, or "the original people." Europeans later used the words "Ojibwe" and "Chippewa" to refer to the Anishinaabe.

Ojibwe oral **tradition** traces **ancestors** to the east coast. They lived along the Atlantic Ocean near the St. Lawrence River until the 1400s CE. A message from the Creator told the Ojibwe to move to "the land where food grows on water." The Ojibwe traveled through the **Great Lakes** region. Areas of today's Michigan, Minnesota, North Dakota, and Wisconsin became their home. Parts of Canada did as well.

THE LENNI LENAPE

The Ojibwe are one of many Native American nations descended from the Lenni Lenape. Today, the Lenni Lenape are also known as the Delaware.

4

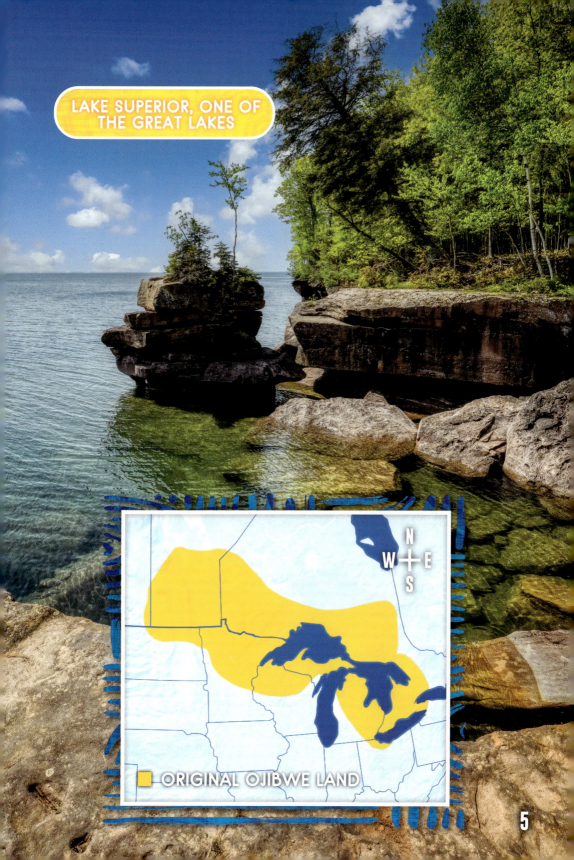

TRADITIONAL OJIBWE LIFE

LEECH LAKE BAND OF OJIBWE ELDER ELAINE FLEMING OFFERING TOBACCO BEFORE A WILD RICE HARVEST

Ancestral Ojibwe lived as the keepers of the natural world. The Ojibwe creation story says that people were created after all other things. They relied on the plants and animals to survive and grow spiritually. They only took what they needed. They offered gifts, often tobacco, as thanks.

Oral tradition has always been how the Ojibwe learn their role as keepers. It is how they share their history and **culture**. Stories often include comparisons to nature as ways to teach important parts of life. The Ojibwe creation story includes the spirit *Waynabozho*. It tells of the creation of Turtle Island, or North America, after a great flood.

CHIEF MEDICINE MAN MQY-MAUSH-KOW SUSH WITH HIS WIFE AND DAUGHTER IN GRAND PORTAGE, MINNESOTA, IN 1936

Family can mean different things to the Ojibwe. It can include animals and plants. It can also include nations **descended** from their ancestors. These nations include the Ottawa, Blackfeet, and many others.

The traditional Ojibwe family is the *dodaim*, or totem. This is how **clans** are organized. A person's clan is based on their father. Each clan serves a special role in traditional Ojibwe society. For example, people in the crane clan often learn to be leaders. People go to Elders in the crane clan for advice.

SEVEN GENERATIONS

Ojibwe leaders consider the future when making decisions. They make decisions based on how they would affect seven generations into the future.

OJIBWE CLANS

CRANE CLAN OR LOON CLAN: LEADERS

BEAR CLAN: PROTECTORS

TURTLE CLAN: HEALERS

MARTIN CLAN: HUNTERS

CATFISH CLAN: TEACHERS

The daily life of ancestral Ojibwe was largely based on the seasons. Families left their winter camps each spring to tap maple trees. Women screwed spouts into the trees to collect sap. They made maple sugar that they stored in birch-bark containers. **Bands** often gathered in large groups each summer. They planted gardens, gathered food, built canoes, and prepared for colder months.

COLLECTING SAP FROM A MAPLE TREE

ILLUSTRATION OF A WILD RICE HARVEST

The wild rice harvest took place in autumn. This grain was an important food throughout the year. In winter, families returned to their winter camps. Men hunted and trapped. Women processed meat and hides.

EUROPEAN CONTACT

FURS FROM THE CANADIAN FUR TRADE AT FORT WILLIAM HISTORICAL PARK

The Ojibwe were well established in the Great Lakes region when they first met the French in the 1600s. They formed a strong trade relationship. The Ojibwe moved westward into Dakota lands as traders wanted more furs. This began a conflict between the two nations that lasted from the 1730s to the 1850s. The Ojibwe pushed the Dakota people farther west.

Britain took control of the Great Lakes region in 1763. The Ojibwe were treated poorly. They did not trust Britain. But many Ojibwe also feared Americans would take their lands. They sided with Britain in the **Revolutionary War** and the **War of 1812**.

PAINTING OF THE BATTLE OF LAKE ERIE DURING THE WAR OF 1812

CHIEF SHINGABA W'OSSIN WHO FOUGHT WITH BRITAIN IN THE WAR OF 1812

GOVERNMENT BOARDING SCHOOL AT LAC DU FLAMBEAU

The Ojibwe and other Native American nations experienced a period of **treaties** and land loss after the wars. The United States forced the Ojibwe to give up large areas of land in the Treaties of 1837 and 1842. But the Ojibwe fought to make sure they were allowed to hunt, fish, and gather on the land.

The U.S. and Canadian governments worked to destroy Ojibwe culture and rights. They pushed the Ojibwe onto **reservations** starting in the 1850s. They forced Ojibwe children into **boarding schools**. They tried to make children unlearn Ojibwe culture. But the Ojibwe never stopped fighting.

U.S. CITIZENS

Many Ojibwe people served in World War I. The Indian Citizenship Act of 1924 was passed to recognize their efforts. It let Native Americans become U.S. citizens. Many Ojibwe people also served in World War II.

FAMOUS OJIBWE

WINONA LaDUKE

BIRTHDAY August 18, 1959

FAMOUS FOR

An Ojibwe activist and author who helps Native Americans gain control of their homelands and restore their cultures

LIFE TODAY

The Ojibwe nation is one of the largest Native American nations in the U.S. There are 20 bands recognized by the U.S. government. They are in Michigan, Minnesota, Montana, North Dakota, and Wisconsin. There are also bands in Canada.

Many bands have been able to secure reservations on their ancestral lands in the U.S. Other bands have land on reservations they share with other Native American nations. Ojibwe descendants live and work on reservations. However, there are many that live throughout the U.S. and the world.

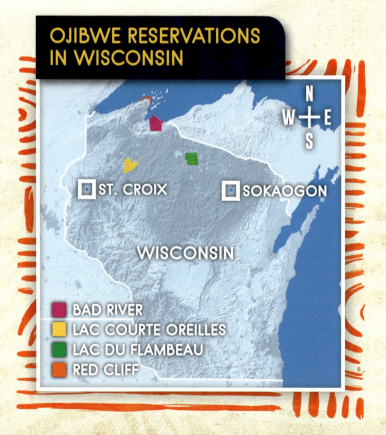

OJIBWE RESERVATIONS IN WISCONSIN

- ST. CROIX
- SOKAOGON

WISCONSIN

- BAD RIVER
- LAC COURTE OREILLES
- LAC DU FLAMBEAU
- RED CLIFF

16

Ancestral Ojibwe communities made decisions based on general agreements. Today, many of the nation's tribal governments are made up of different branches. They work for members of their bands. Some governments have tribal **councils** or similar committees that make laws.

GOVERNMENT OF THE LEECH LAKE BAND OF OJIBWE

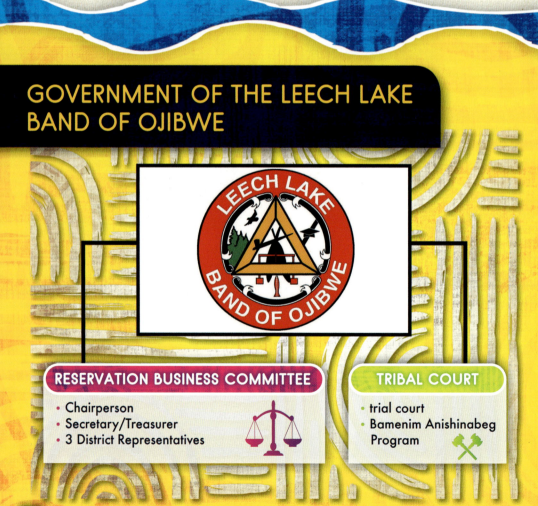

Many Ojibwe governments provide social services to band members. Services include community development and a police force. Some also provide family, health, and educational services. They help members learn and live well.

CONTINUING TRADITIONS

OJIBWE LANGUAGE STUDY GROUP AT THE UNIVERSITY OF MICHIGAN

The Ojibwe are working to educate their community about traditional practices. One of the ways they keep their culture alive is through language. There are many language programs throughout the nation. An Ojibwe language institute is in Hayward, Wisconsin. Students learn the language in both the classroom and through traditional activities such as maple sugaring.

The Mille Lacs Band of Ojibwe offers an Ojibwe Language and Culture Program at its schools. Elders share their knowledge with students. Some Elders also teach traditional crafts at the Mille Lacs Indian Museum in Minnesota.

MILLE LACS INDIAN MUSEUM IN MINNESOTA

SPEAKER FROM THE LAC LA CROIX FIRST NATION TEACHING STORYTELLING

MAKING MAPLE SUGAR ON THE BAD RIVER BAND OF LAKE SUPERIOR CHIPPEWA RESERVATION

Many Ojibwe participate in other traditional practices. Some bands provide classes that teach Ojibwe skills such as tanning hides and canoe making. People also practice traditional food collection. Maple sugaring is commonly practiced in the spring. People collect wild rice along the waterways of Minnesota and Wisconsin each autumn.

The Mādahòkì Farm is in Ontario, Canada. It has festivals that celebrate Native American cultures. It hosts activities and events year-round. The farm is also home to a herd of Ojibwe Spirit Horses. The Ojibwe Cultural Foundation is also in Ontario. It has classes, workshops, and events. Visitors can view Ojibwe art at the museum.

CANOE MAKING

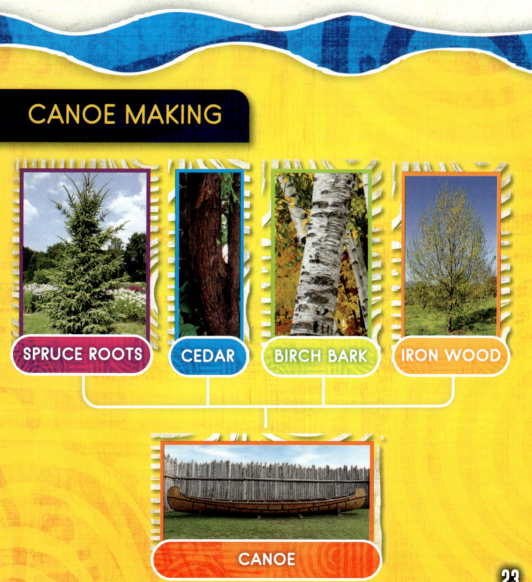

SPRUCE ROOTS · CEDAR · BIRCH BARK · IRON WOOD → CANOE

FIGHT TODAY, BRIGHT TOMORROW

The Ojibwe have fought to maintain their culture despite the **colonization** of North America. Today, wild rice is at risk. Harvests have sharply declined. One major threat is **climate change**. Wild rice needs a hard winter freeze to grow. But wild rice habitats have been experiencing warmer winters. **Invasive species** also harm wild rice.

Wild rice beds are harmed by direct human activities. Building homes along lakeshores disturbs beds. Boating can break the plants. Dams change water levels and affect plant growth. Mining adds salts to the water that can kill wild rice.

WILD RICE

HARVESTING WILD RICE

SACRED FOOD

The Ojibwe word for wild rice is *manoomin*.

WILD RICE

The Ojibwe are trying to protect wild rice. They are trying to stop harmful mining projects. Some gather to speak up against mining. The Mille Lacs Band of Ojibwe created Water Over Nickel in 2023. This program teaches people how nickel mining harms wild rice and human health. It aims to stop more nickel mines from being built.

The nation is also finding ways to improve wild rice growth. Ojibwe Elders and environmental scientists are working together to create solutions. Using traditional knowledge along with modern science may help bring some balance back to the natural world!

FOOD THREAT

Fish are a traditional food for the Ojibwe. The nation has treaty rights to fish in parts of the Great Lakes and other waterways. But increasing amounts of harmful chemicals are now found in fish from these areas. This can lead to major health problems in the Ojibwe people.

TIMELINE

1693
Madeline Island becomes the center of the Ojibwe Nation

BY THE 1400s
Ojibwe peoples travel from the Atlantic coast to the Great Lakes region

1941
After the attack on Pearl Harbor during World War II, Ojibwe men begin enlisting in the U.S. military as Code Talkers

1600s
Ojibwe peoples begin trading furs with the French

BETWEEN 1836 AND 1867
The Ojibwe experience a period of great change and hardship as the core of their land is taken from them by the U.S. and Canadian governments through treaties

1989

Winona LaDuke starts the White Earth Land Recovery Project to help return land to the Ojibwe

2021

Ojibwe peoples gather in Minnesota to oppose the building of the Line 3 pipeline project that would damage natural resources

1968

The American Indian Movement is founded to fight for sovereignty, culture recognition, and civil and human rights

2010

The Fond du Lac Band of Lake Superior Chippewa makes Ojibwemowin the official language of the band

1995

Professor John Nichols and Professor Earl Nyholm from the University of Minnesota co-author *A Concise Dictionary of Minnesota Ojibwe*

GLOSSARY

ancestors—relatives who lived long ago

bands—groups of people who live as communities and share a culture

boarding schools—schools created throughout the 1800s to remove traditional Native American ways of life and replace them with American culture

clans—groups of people who share common ancestors

climate change—a human-caused change in Earth's weather due to warming temperatures

colonization—the act of taking over another nation for power

councils—groups of people who meet to run governments

culture—the beliefs, arts, and ways of life in a place or society

descended—came from a person or group of people who lived at an earlier time

Great Lakes—large freshwater lakes on the border between Canada and the United States; the Great Lakes are Superior, Michigan, Ontario, Erie, and Huron.

invasive species—plants or animals that are not originally from the area; invasive species often cause harm to their new environments.

reservations—lands set aside by the U.S. government for the forced removal of Native American communities from their original lands; reservations formed by the Canadian government are called reserves.

Revolutionary War—the war between 1775 and 1783 in which the United States fought for independence from Great Britain

tradition—a custom, idea, or belief handed down from one generation to the next

treaties—official agreements between two groups

War of 1812—the second war between the United States and Great Britain largely based on disagreements over trade

TO LEARN MORE

AT THE LIBRARY

Erdrich, Louise. *The Birchbark House*. New York, N.Y.: Harper, 2024.

Havrelock, Deidre. *Indigenous Ingenuity: A Celebration of Traditional North American Knowledge*. New York, N.Y.: Little, Brown, and Company, 2023.

Vukelich Kaagegaabaw, James. *Wisdom Weavers: Explore the Ojibwe Language and the Meaning of Dream Catchers*. New York, N.Y.: Becker&Meyer! Kids, 2024.

ON THE WEB

FACTSURFER

Factsurfer.com gives you a safe, fun way to find more information.

1. Go to www.factsurfer.com.
2. Enter "the Ojibwe" into the search box and click 🔍.
3. Select your book cover to see a list of related content.

INDEX

bands, 10, 16, 18, 19, 21, 22, 26
boarding schools, 14
Canadian government, 14
canoe making, 10, 22, 23
clans, 8, 9
climate change, 24
colonization, 24
councils, 18
culture, 4, 6, 7, 10, 11, 14, 20, 21, 23, 24
Dakota, 12
dodaim, 8, 10, 11
Elders, 6, 8, 21, 26
food, 10, 11, 20, 22, 24, 25, 26, 27
future, 9, 26
government of the Leech Lake Band of Ojibwe, 18
Great Lakes, 4, 5, 12, 13, 27
history, 4, 6, 7, 10, 11, 12, 13, 14, 15, 18, 26
homeland, 4, 5, 13, 14, 16
Indian Citizenship Act of 1924, 15
LaDuke, Winona, 15
language, 4, 20, 21, 25
Leech Lake Band of Ojibwe, 6, 18, 19
Lenni Lenape, 4
Mādahòkì Farm, 23
map, 5, 16
members, 18, 19
Mille Lacs Band of Ojibwe, 21, 26
Mille Lacs Indian Museum, 21
name, 4
Ojibwe Cultural Foundation, 23
Ojibwe Language and Culture Program, 21
reservations, 14, 16, 22
seven generations, 9
timeline, 28–29
traditions, 4, 6, 7, 8, 9, 20, 21, 22, 23, 26, 27
treaties, 14, 27
U.S. government, 14, 16
wars, 12, 13, 14, 15
Water Over Nickel, 26
wild rice, 6, 11, 22, 24, 25, 26

The images in this book are reproduced through the courtesy of: Ross D. Franklin/ AP Images, cover; Michael Siluk/ Alamy, p. 3; unknown/ Wikipedia, pp. 4, 18; Jim Schwabel, pp. 4-5, 28 (1963); Jessie Wardarski/ AP Images, p. 6; Dave Jonasen, p. 7; Historical/ Contributor/ Getty Images, p. 8; Joe Ferrer, p. 9 (crane); Ronald Wittek, p. 9 (bear); Agami Photo Agency, p. 9 (martin); Brian Lasenby, p. 9 (turtle); Eric Engbretson/ U.S. Fish and Wildlife Service/ Wikipedia, p. 9 (catfish); Roland Reed/ Wikipedia, p. 10; Seth Eastman/ Library of Congress, p. 11; All Canada Photos/ Alamy, p. 12; Science History Images/ Alamy, p. 13; Charles King Bird/ Smithsonian American Art Museum, p. 13 (Chief Shingaba W'ossin); Jeff the quiet/ wikipedia, p. 14; unknown/ mnopedia, p. 15 (U.S. citizens); ZUMA Press Inc/ Alamy, pp. 15 (Winona LaDuke), 24-25; Big Joe, pp. 16-17; Matt Hahnewald Photography/ Alamy, p. 17; Myotus/ Wikipedia, pp. 19, 21 (Mille Lacs Indian Museum); Forest Service, Eastern Region/ Flickr, p. 19 (Ojibwe Chairman Faron Jackson); Tony Ding/ AP Images, p. 20; Stacy Bengs/ AP Images, p. 21 (storytelling); Mary Annette Pember/ AP Images, p. 22; Irina Borsuchenko, p. 23 (spruce roots); USDA-NRCS PLANTS Database/ Wikipedia, p. 23 (cedar); Danita Delimont, p. 23 (birch bark); it:Jon Benedictus, p. 23 (iron wood); Melissa Kopka, pp. 23, 31; Dave Orrick/ AP Images, p. 24; Karel Bock, p. 26; Jacob Boomsma/ Alamy, p. 27; Stephen Taylor/ Alamy, p. 28 (1600s); NurPhoto SRL/ Alamy, p. 29 (2021).